Major H. C. HARRISON, D.S.O.
JULY 1915. – 22/12/16

Major A. E. RANN, M.B.E., M.C.
22/12/16—20/7/17

BATTERY COMMANDERS
OF
71st (SOUTH AFRICAN)
SIEGE BATTERY

Major P. N. G. FITZPATRICK
20/7/17—14/12/17

Major E. H. TAMPLIN, M.C
14/12/17—11/11/18

A HISTORY OF THE SEVENTY-FIRST SIEGE BATTERY SOUTH AFRICAN HEAVY ARTILLERY

From July, 1915, the date of its formation at Cape Town, to the 11th November, 1918, when "Cease Fire!" sounded at Lesdain, on the Escault Canal, near Tournai, Belgium

The Naval & Military Press Ltd

in association with

The Imperial War Museum
Department of Printed Books

Published jointly by

The Naval & Military Press Ltd

Unit 10 Ridgewood Industrial Park,

Uckfield, East Sussex,

TN22 5QE England

Tel: +44 (0) 1825 749494

Fax: +44 (0) 1825 765701

www.naval–military–press.com

www.military-genealogy.com

and

The Imperial War Museum, London

Department of Printed Books

www.iwm.org.uk

The 71st (South African) Siege Battery

Dedicates

This little history to those of its members who fell in the execution of their duty and in the cause of Freedom and Justice.

We leave their bodies to the kindly land of France. Their memories are our own. Their lonely graves will never be really lonely. Often in spirit will we tread the Battlefields where our good comrades rest. Often, in far South Africa, round warm firesides, we will name their names. And when the cold winds blow and the rains descend, we will rejoin them, Souls that have touched are never parted. The Spirit that was the Battery will not die.

These, our departed comrades, for us are yet alive, and so we would have their dear ones regard them. They fell in Freedom's cause, and no true man hereafter will deny them envy.

FOREWORD.

HE weary weeks of waiting for demobilisation have furnished an opportunity for the collection of material for this little work, which is intended to give a brief outline of the activities of the 71st (South African) Siege Battery, from the time it went into position at Mailly-Maillet on the Somme in April, 1916, until the 11th November, 1918, the date of the Armistice, when the Battery was in Belgium some 40 kilometres West of Mons.

Difficulties have been encountered in gathering accurate particulars and dates, but if the result serves in later years to bring back memories to those who were on the spot, and even supply recollections to those who were never there, its purpose will have been achieved.

Some may hold the opinion that too much space has been devoted to the events of 1918, but it is only natural that the events of the past year come back more readily and in fuller detail than earlier occurrences, while the operations culminating in the Battle of Givenchy on the 18th April, 1918, were some of the most critical in the whole War, and the repulse of the enemy on that date was probably the turning point in the fortunes of the Allies. It is a matter for regret that it has not been possible to publish a full list of casualties in this unofficial publication, but as the full particulars are no longer with the Battery records, it has been considered advisable to refrain from printing a detailed casualty list.

The South African Heavy Artillery Brigade

In support of the German South West African campaign in 1914-15 a Heavy Artillery Brigade, armed with 4.7 and 4-inch naval guns, was formed at Cape Town, under the command of Colonel Rose, Royal Marine Artillery. A number of Imperial non-commissioned officers, drawn from the Royal Marine Artillery, formed the nucleus of the unit, and most of the personnel were recruited from various South African Artillery Regiments.

□ □

The Regiment of South African Heavy Artillery

On the conclusion of the German South West African Campaign in July, 1915, the Brigade was disbanded, and in the same month a Regiment of Heavy Artillery was recruited for service overseas from the principal centres of the union. The senior officers and non-commissioned officers at this, the date of the formation of the Regiment, were, as in the case of the Heavy Artillery Brigade, Imperial men, the rest of the personnel being largely composed of ex-members of the Heavy Artillery Brigade. Men of fine physique and a standard height of five feet eight inches only were accepted. The roll was finally closed when a total of Six hundred men was reached and these formed the first representative contingent to leave South Africa for overseas. All subsequent recruits for this Regiment served as reinforcing drafts to the original force and were called for from time to time as found necessary.

The personnel of the five batteries recruited represented respectively :—

1. The Western Cape Province.
2. The Eastern Cape Province.
3. The Transvaal.
4. Kimberley and the Diamond Districts.
5. The Province of Natal.

The Regiment sailed from Cape Town at 6 p.m. on Saturday, the 28th August, 1915, and landed at Plymouth on the 15th September, 1915. The formation of the Batteries was completed during the voyage. The Regiment proceeded from Plymouth to Cooden Camp, Bexhill-on-Sea, which was reached on the night of the 15th September, 1915, when the officers, non-commissioned officers and men of the five batteries were granted fourteen days' disembarkation leave.

□ □

No. 3 (Transvaal) Battery
South African Heavy Artillery

On the return from leave of the officers, non-commissioned officers and men at the end of September, the Battery was engaged at Cooden in general training and equipping, and the following officers were posted to it :—

Captain H. C. Harrison, Commanding Officer.
Captain A. E. Rann, Second in Command.
Second-Lieutenant P. N. G. Fitzpatrick.
Second-Lieutenant E. Mason.
Second-Lieutenant A. B. Crump.

During October the senior officers proceeded to Lydd to undergo a course of Gunnery, on completion of which Captain Harrison was promoted to the rank of Major.

71st (South African) Siege Battery Royal Garrison Artillery

During October, 1915, the War Office decided to rate the South African Regiment of Heavy Artillery as Siege Artillery and No 3 (Transvaal) Battery became the 71st (South African) Siege Battery, Royal Garrison Artillery. The Batteries were permitted to retain their South African cap badge and their identity as South African Heavy Artillery.

While at Cooden Camp the members of the South African Batteries were the recipients of much hospitality and kindness from the inhabitants of Bexhill-on-Sea and will always remember with gratitude their very enjoyable stay there.

The Battery proceeded to Lydd Training Camp on the 28th December, 1915, for the purpose of carrying out the necessary practice shoots before embarking for France. Much to the disappointment of all concerned an outbreak of measles in the Battery necessitated their going into quarantine for seven weeks and delayed the time, so keenly anticipated, when they would prove in practice what their training had been worth.

On the 1st January, 1916, Bombardiers E. A. Mitchell and A. W. F. Roper were granted commissions, the former being posted to the 71st, and the latter to the 74th (South African) Siege Batteries, and on the 15th April, 1916, Bombardier R. S. Miller was granted a commission and posted to the 125th (South African) Siege Battery.

The practice shooting at Lydd was carried out on 8-inch Rifled Muzzle Loaders and 9.45-inch Howitzers of an Austrian pattern. The Battery, with the other South African Batteries, was, on conclusion thereof, armed with four 6-inch 26-cwt. Breech Loading Howitzers. These were among the first of this type of weapon to be issued, and on the arrival of the Battery in France became an object of considerable interest to officers of other units, who were usually anxious to see this new piece of ordnance operating under war conditions.

The Battery mobilised at Fareham on the 6th April, 1916, took over its guns, equipment and transport column, left for France via Southampton on the 15th, arrived at Le Havre on the 16th, and remained at Rest Camp until the 20th idem, when it proceeded by rail to Beauquesne.

From the latter place the guns were taken to Rancheval, while the personnel went forward to prepare positions in Mailly-Maillet in anticipation of the impending offensive on the Somme.

The men were at this time billeted in farm-houses and the battery position was situated on the outskirts of a wood amid picturesque surroundings. These conditions were extremely unlike what had been anticipated by those new to France. The cultivated fields, compact houses filled with women and children, the estaminets and village shops, formed a strange setting for a battery position. It had yet to be learnt that very often these apparently peaceful scenes were liable to rude interruption at any moment by hostile bombardment, and that the presence of French women and children was not only no guarantee of quiet uneventful days, but that, with a bravery and tenacity of purpose, perhaps unparalleled in the history of the world, these people remained in their houses even when the enemy shell-fire had left little else than ruined cottages with perhaps a cellar to live in. The French Government was, in fact, frequently compelled to take active measures to ensure their removal from the more dangerous areas.

Commanded by Major Harrison, and attached to the VIIIth corps, the Battery came into action on the 25th May, 1916. The guns were registered and thereafter the Battery remained silent until it might be required for the impending Somme push ; the period of waiting was occupied in improving the position. It was not, however, fated to commence its career in this position, being suddenly ordered on the 2nd June, 1916, to Ypres, to assist in a Canadian counter-attack to recover important trenches at Hooge, which had recently been lost. The Battery reached the city of Ypres on the 4th, and at once pulled into action, under heavy hostile fire, sustaining in so doing its first casualties. Lieutenant Mason was seriously injured, and of other ranks two were killed and five were wounded. The Battery remained in action in its position near the Dixmude Gate on the Northern edge of the city until the 14th. During this baptismal period it was practically continuously in action, for most of the time under heavy hostile shelling, and lost five men killed and twenty-two wounded. Eleven thousand shells were fired in six days, and No. 1. gun on one occasion fired eighty-one rounds in twenty-nine minutes, which probably constitutes a record for this type of artillery, as the handling of eight thousand one hundred pounds of metal by any one gun team in twenty-nine minutes required an almost super-human effort, especially when the fact is taken into consideration that the Battery as a whole, during the period of six days including the above operation, had thrown one million one hundred thousand pounds weight of metal into the enemy's lines and suffered thirty-two casualties out of a total personnel of one hundred and fifty.

A Four-Wheeled Drive pulling a gun into position.   German Retreat, October, 1918

The whole operation was very successful and the 71st Siege Battery was, at Godewaersvelde, thanked in person by General Currie, then in command of the Canadian Corps, for the valuable assistance rendered. Battery Sergeant-Major S. G. Dacombe was awarded the Distinguished Conduct Medal for his services in this operation.

Lieutenant Levy was transferred from the 44th Brigade and joined the Battery during its stay at Ypres.

On the 18th June the Battery returned to its position at Mailly-Maillet and preparation for the Somme offensive was resumed.

Preliminary bombardment of an intense nature commenced on the 25th June and continued until July 1st, when the grand attack was launched and the Battery was heavily in action, being called upon at one time to fire at "gun fire" rate for sixty-five minutes. The Battery moved forward on the 5th and occupied a position at Becordel, from which it participated in the battles for Mametz Wood, Ovillers, and Contalmaison.

During their stay at Becordel the Battery personnel lived in canvas shelters in the vicinity of the guns. At this stage of the war the necessity for concealing gun positions from visual and enemy aircraft observations had not yet been universally recognised. The art of camouflage was still in its infancy and had not yet come into its own.

On the 28th July, Major Harrison was awarded the Distinguished Service Order and Bombardier H. E. B. Robinson the Military Medal, for reconnaissance operations during the battle of Pozières.

Throughout the whole offensive on the Somme, Major Harrison's work was largely instrumental in gaining for the Battery the reputation for successful shooting. He carried out several important reconnaissances, notably in Pozières, which was at that time "No Man's Land." Captain Rann, who was then carrying out the duties of forward observation officer, also did excellent work, leaving the Battery before dawn and returning well after sundown, day after day.

The signallers, whose ranks had been seriously depleted, were practically continuously employed, as exceptionally long lines of communication had to be maintained between the battery position and the observation posts, frequently necessitating the repair of lines under heavy shell fire and trying conditions generally.

It was from the position at Becordel also, that the Battery participated in the attack on Courcellette, Martinpuich and Flers, on the 15th September, 1916, when the tanks were used for the first time with such wonderful advantage.

A further forward movement took place to Bazentin on the 20th September, when Major Harrison rejoined the Battery from hospital where he had been under treatment for gas, and here, as at earlier positions, the men lived in small shacks near the guns.

Bazentin is memorable by reason of the general conditions, which were probably the most trying experienced in the history of the Battery. Rain had fallen incessantly since the middle of July and the heavy clay soil in this district clung to everything. The work on the drag-ropes in pulling out the guns on the completion of shoots was consequently very heavy and tested the staying power and morale of the gunners, who were on the guns day and night, well-nigh to breaking point. The oozing mud around Ypres was bad, but was scarcely as heart-breaking as the heavy mud now experienced. The roads were execrable, lorries were frequently ditched, and ammunition had to be carried a considerable distance to the guns. The new 106 fuze, which is extremely sensitive, causing immediate detonation of the shell on the slightest impact, and consequently of immense value when firing on moving or similar targets, was first brought into use at Bazentin, and was thereafter very frequently employed.

The casualties suffered in this position amounted to four men killed and seven wounded, while Lieutenant Levy had to return to England owing to sickness. At this opportune time the first men to be granted "Blighty" leave left the Battery.

The Battery was principally engaged on trench shooting during this period. Among special operations allotted to the Battery at Bazentin was the task of clearing out a bombing stop in the Regina Trench, which had been partially occupied by our infantry, but whose further progress was held up by persistent bombing. In order to clear the remainder of the trench all infantry were withdrawn to communication and support trenches, while Captain Rann, accompanied by two signallers, went forward, and from a point in the occupied portion of the trench, barely fifty yards from the target, on two consecutive days controlled the fire of the Battery which was concentrated on that part of the trench still in enemy hands. Captain Rann and his party were covered by a heavy machine gun fire on the enemy, but, owing to their proximity to the target, were exposed to a considerable risk from our own guns, and in recognition of their services Captain Rann was awarded the Military Cross and Bombardier G. W. Munro, Gunners J. H. M. Turnbull and G. T. B. Tasker each received the Military Medal.

On the 22nd December, 1916, the Battery moved to Beauval on rest, and Major Harrison, still suffering from the effects of gas, left for England, leaving Captain Rann in command.

The Battery position was now within easy reach of Amiens, one of the finest cities in Northern France, and at that time full of the gay life which affords so much needed a contrast to existence under war conditions. Every opportunity of visiting the town and enjoying a few hours of refreshing relaxation was eagerly seized by all.

A return to the line was made on the 2nd January, 1917, when the Battery went into action at Ovillers, which had formed a part of the German front line system before the battle, and where the conditions with regard to mud were found to be little better than those at Bazentin, although the roads approaching the position were certainly kept in a better state. At this place box-respirators were issued to the Battery for the first time to safeguard the personnel against gas attacks, steel helmets as a protection from shrapnel having been issued earlier at Ypres. The necessity for making some provision against the shocking weather conditions had apparently been realised, and in consequence Nissen huts were issued by the authorities for housing the personnel. Owing to a shortage of South African officers, Second-Lieutenant W. J. Davies, Royal Garrison Artillery, was attached to the Battery on the 3rd January.

Successful operations were carried out from this position by Lieutenant Mitchell, who observed for important shoots from one of our advanced listening posts.

From the 1st January, 1917, the pay of the South African Heavy Artillery Batteries, which had previously been at Imperial rates, was increased to Union Defence Force rates, the difference being paid by the Union Government. An allowance of two shillings *per diem* was also granted to signallers from the same date.

At Ovillers little other than trench targets were fired on. The incessant frost, which lasted from early in January until the close of February, necessitated the maintenance day and night of braziers under the guns to prevent the oil in the recoil mechanism from freezing. The severity of the weather resulted in a good deal of sickness among the men, rendering it difficult at times to carry on with depleted gun crews. Moreover, so hard had the frozen ground become that it was no uncommon sight to see the spade of the trail buckle up when the gun recoiled, a difficulty frequently experienced at this time by siege batteries. In addition to these hardships water became exceedingly scarce, and it was often necessary to break the ice in the surrounding shell holes in order to have the morning wash. Often, also, water from frozen shell holes had to be used for making tea and generally for cooking purposes.

In February, 1917, Lieutenant Crump was transferred to the 73rd

(South African) Siege Battery with the rank of Captain, and Bombardier J. C. Watters and Corporal A. P. Green were transferred from that Battery to the 71st with the rank of Second-Lieutenant. Similarly Bombardier Bower of this Battery was, on appointment to commissioned rank, posted to the 75th (South African) Siege Battery.

On the 8th March two guns were moved to Thiepval in order to partake in the Loupart Wood and Miraimont operations. Just before the attack was due, the enemy commenced his great retreat to the Hindenburg Line, and the 71st Siege Battery was among those which followed on his heels as closely as possible, going into action at Ervillers and Mory, and eventually, early in July, reaching the Hindenburg Line at Croisilles.

On the 17th March—the second day of the retreat—Captain Rann was slightly and Lieutenant Mitchell severely wounded while engaged in making a forward reconnaissance.

A move forward was made on the 22nd March with all four guns, the intention being to strike, at Pozières, the main Albert-Bapaume Road—the only one in the forward area whose condition permitted the transport of heavy artillery. Three of the guns were unfortunately ditched before arriving at Pozières, and only one reached the main road, where it followed the stream of traffic going forward, and went straight-way into action at Ervillers on the 23rd. It fired on the villages of Croisilles and Ecoust in front of the Hindenburg Line, causing some surprise to the enemy, who evidently had not expected heavy guns to be brought up so promptly. It was impossible to bring up the remaining three guns until the 3rd April, owing to the Albert-Bapaume Road having been temporarily closed to enable very necessary repairs to be effected.

The weather continued severe and blizzards were frequent, while the destruction of all buildings and material by the enemy during his retirement increased the hardships of the advance, the gunners having to procure what shelter they could from tarpaulins and trench covers.

The Battery was constantly engaging enemy troops fighting rear-guard actions in the villages of St. Leger and Ecoust, which they held for a time with great tenacity, but were eventually forced to evacuate.

The first battle of Bullecourt opened on 17th April, 1917, by which time all our heavy guns were in position, and a strong attack protected by a very effective barrage was launched on the enemy's lines. Its

The "Woahs" and "Narks." Mory. April, 1917

"Mory Church" as left by the Huns. Somme Retreat of 1917

intensity and the number of guns it had been possible to bring up into action must have caused him considerable surprise. Very bitter fighting ensued on that day, which heralded the commencement of a series of intense encounters, right up to the second battle of Bullecourt on the 3rd May.

At this time each battery established and maintained its own observation posts in the forward area, and the 71st Siege Battery was particularly fortunate, when in position at Mory, in securing a post known as "C.I.a." on a hill in front of Bullecourt, commanding an extensive view of the surrounding country, and from which the construction of what subsequently proved to be the famous Drocourt-Queant switch line was observed. The unique situation of this post rendered it possible to overlook the position of practically every hostile battery within range, and offered excellent opportunities for useful counter-battery work, which was extensively carried out particularly at a later date from the Croisilles position. One hostile battery in position near Riencourt is called to mind in this connection. It was in the habit of firing into St. Leger or harassing the roads in that vicinity, but as the flash of each gun could be clearly seen by the forward observation officer, it was consequently an easy matter to open up with a neutralising fire on every occasion it became active. Other targets comprised stretches of wire protecting the Hindenburg Line, and such places of interest and importance as "The Knuckle," "The Hump" and Bullecourt were frequently fired upon, while the strong emplacements on the Hindenburg Line known as "Gog" and "Magog" frequently received attention from the forward observation officers, for whom they constituted very interesting targets.

Only one casualty was sustained at Mory. While at that position Lieutenant Lawlor and Second-Lieutenant Henderson joined the Battery from the Base depôt, and Gunner P. D. Waller, then serving as Battery Commander's assistant, was promoted to commissioned rank and remained with the Battery.

On the 4th July, a position at Croisilles, only two thousand yards from the Hindenburg Line, was occupied with two guns, from which practically every hostile battery and position of fighting importance on that front could be reached. The other two guns were brought up some days later, and pulled into position at a distance of some six hundred yards in rear of the forward section.

The Battery, controlled from "C.I.a." observation post, was constantly able to do excellent work, chiefly of a counter-battery nature, but in addition every movement of enemy troops observed was immediately engaged. The latter targets always appealed more to the gun-layers and the crews generally, as it was upon their speed and ability that effective shooting so much depended, and as nothing was so conducive to a lack of keenness and a loss of interest as the large amount of "blind" shooting which crews were so often called upon to do.

The battery position was good, and men were safely housed in a tunnel cut into a bank and in dug-outs sunk into the ground after the German pattern. Despite frequent hostile shelling, the only casualties suffered were three killed and seven wounded, which numbers would inevitably have been greatly exceeded but for the protection afforded by the site of the gun-pits, admirably sheltered by a bank, and the dug-outs. Lieutenants Levy and Roper joined here from England.

On the 20th July, during the progress of a hostile destructive shoot on the forward section of the Battery, Major Rann, who had immediately gone forward to see that the men were safeguarded as far as possible, was wounded, and on this occasion one of the guns was put out of action by a direct hit. Captain Fitzpatrick assumed command of the Battery.

The most important fighting in which the Battery was engaged from this position was that involved in the battles of Bullecourt in the attempt to break the Hindenburg Line.

The living quarters at Croisilles consisted of bivouacs and huts away from the guns, and as there were plenty of well-stocked canteens in the neighbourhood, the men lived well and were very comfortable, while occasional visits to Amiens served for relaxation, and generally speaking greater opportunities for sport and recreation were offered and eagerly seized.

In addition, the system of sending men away on rest for fourteen days to St. Valery-sur-Somme, a very pleasant Rest Camp, was here first introduced.

Lieutenant Lawlor was transferred to the 73rd Siege Battery on the 25th July, 1917, with the rank of Captain.

It became apparent at this time that the enemy had been studying the counter-battery tactics adopted by the Allies earlier in the year during the offensive on the Somme, and was now employing similar methods with a view to neutralising our fire as much as possible.

On the 31st August, 1917, one section of the Battery pulled out, and for the second time in its history went north to Ypres to take over

One of our "12 inch" shell holes.   Bazentin, October, 1916

from a section of the 301st Siege Battery. The position was just outside the famous Menin Gate.

The battle of Ypres was found to be in full swing, and on the second day after its arrival the section was subjected to a heavy gas bombardment resulting in sixty casualties. The second section followed, after being relieved by the 301st Siege Battery, and arrived at Ypres on the 15th September. The men here lived in the Haune Works on the outer ramparts of the city, which had been constructed several centuries earlier. These billets were far from healthy, but were necessary on account of the cover afforded, which, although scanty, was preferable to living in the open.

During a period of great activity the Battery participated in the battles of Frezenberg Ridge on the 9th September, Vampire and Boiry Farms on the 20th, Zonnebeke on the 26th, and Broedseinde and Passchendalle on the 4th October.

Corporal E. Naitby was awarded the Military Medal for the manner in which, during the heavy shelling of the Menin Gate position by high velocity guns, he successfully extinguished a dump of ammunition which had caught alight.

All these actions were highly successful and it is of interest to note that on the 20th September the Battery supported the 9th Division, to which the South African Infantry was attached, for the first and only time during the war. The South African Infantry had been engaged in the capture of the Butte de Warlencourt on the Somme while the Battery was at Bazentin, but were to the left of the sector covered by the Battery.

The Battery moved on the 28th September to a position at Cavalry Farm, and on the 5th October again advanced to Bavaria House, in which position it was subjected to heavy shelling, losing in a period of fourteen days four men killed and twenty-five wounded.

It was while in position at Bavaria House that for the first time rear billets were provided to ensure that the gun crews, when off duty, secured the much needed rest and sleep which it was practically impossible to obtain at the battery position. The first billets selected were the Ypres ramparts, which, although far from comfortable as they were invariably very damp, nevertheless afforded the only safe shelter available. This, however, necessitated a march of five or six kilometres through continuous mud and slush to reach the Battery at Bavaria House, the route to which was frequently subjected to heavy harassing fire by hostile batteries.

19

On the 18th October, Lieutenant Watters, who was conducting a forward reconnaissance on Abraham Heights, was forced, with the two signallers accompanying him, to take cover in a concrete "pill-box" owing to the intensity of hostile shelling. A few minutes later a shell burst in the entrance of the shelter, killing five and wounding four of the nine occupants. Lieutenant Watters was so severely wounded that he succumbed on the following day. The two signallers with him were seriously wounded.

The position at Bavaria House could not be considered as a good one as it adjoined both a Decauville junction and cross-roads, and was in consequence frequently subjected to the heavy harassing fire of enemy batteries, one gun being put out of action and ammunition set alight, but the concentration of our artillery rendered it impossible to obtain a better site at the time. The surrounding country was one vast mud swamp rendering the approaches to the Battery very difficult, and the work in the gun-pits was carried on under most adverse conditions owing to the presence of standing water often from six to twelve inches in depth. Moreover, the enemy's air craft was exceedingly active rendering his counter-battery work very effective, while the incessant bombing during both day and night by enemy aeroplanes added tremendously to the general strain.

The casualties were so numerous and the gun crews became depleted to such an extent that for a time it was only possible to fight two guns. Great credit is due to the gunners for the almost superhuman efforts necessary to keep the guns in action, and to the signallers, who, reduced to six or seven in number, were kept extremely busy in maintaining telephone communication. Assistance was eventually obtained for a time from 356th Siege Battery, and the New Zealand Infantry were requisitioned for bringing ammunition to the gun-pits. The guns were here fed by light line owing to the impassability of the roads.

Eventually owing to its depleted strength, the Battery was relieved by the 2nd Canadian Siege Battery on the 22nd October, 1917.

While at Ypres Lieutenant Levy was invalided to England owing to ill-health, and Battery Quartermaster-Sergeant White was gassed and also evacuated, his position being filled by the promotion of Sergeant J. Wardrop.

The personnel of the Battery, when relieved, was thoroughly worn out. They had experienced strenuous fighting under the worst conditions, gun teams had been reduced to a minimum, while opportunities for rest and recreation were entirely lacking. For meritorious service during this

The Battery position, "Hauue Works," Menin Gate, Ypres.   September, 1917

period, Second-Lieutenant A. P. Green and Bombardier A. T. Petters were mentioned in despatches.

The Battery pulled out on the 22nd October, 1917, and proceeded to Lievin, staying one night each at Watou and Bruay en route. On the journey the men enjoyed to the full the chance of very welcome relaxation and recreation, and had a particularly good time at Watou.

The position taken over from the 2nd Canadian Siege Battery at Lievin on the 25th October, 1917, proved an excellent one in every respect. A big bank immediately in front of the guns provided very good natural cover and there was a running stream immediately in rear. The men were comfortably housed in cellars near the guns, and had little fighting to do. The targets engaged comprised hostile battery positions for the most part, and barrages were occasionally put up in support of night raids by the Infantry. This new position was in the middle of one of the principal coal districts of France. Visits were frequently made into Bethune, one of the large business centres of the neighbourhood, where excellent shops still carried on under more or less normal conditions, where numerous luxuries could be obtained and English papers and magazines were on sale.

The rest thus enjoyed by the men soon resulted in a complete restoration of physical fitness and a revival of keenness and vigour, which had undergone a heavy strain at Ypres.

The Battery refitted stores and equipment, and the reinforcements necessary to complete the establishment were obtained from the Base depôt.

Suddenly orders came through for the Battery to stand by to be relieved, and at dusk on the evening of the 8th November, the guns were handed over to the 73rd (South African) Siege Battery, and with the latter's guns the Battery, now fully equipped, proceeded to Barlin. Two new pieces were drawn there to ensure the Battery being in the best fighting condition. The next night a move was made into Arras, and from there on the evening of the 10th the Battery, together with five others from the same front, joined the procession of batteries of various calibres moving South along the Arras-Cambrai Road. The string of lorries, tractors and guns, which stretched away into the distance as far as the eye could reach, seemed interminable. Bapaume was reached the same night and billets of a somewhat airy nature occupied among the ruined buildings.

On the 12th a halt was made at Aizecourt-le-Haut on the Peronne-Cambrai Road. The greatest secrecy had been maintained with regard to the entire move, and up to this point the general impression was that the Battery was destined for the Italian Front. Dull, misty weather having prevailed throughout, the possibility of observation by the enemy either from the air or the ground was reduced to a minimum. On the 13th November the guns were pulled into a position on the outskirts of the village of Gouzeaucourt, which was fated a fortnight later to fall into enemy hands. Pursuant on the policy of secrecy, every precaution was taken to conceal all movement on arrival. Extensive camouflage had been spread over the gun-pits, ammunition had been brought up and stacked in the pits before the arrival of the guns, the position had been resected, lines of fire laid out and telephonic communications arranged, but the battery was not allowed to use the latter or register the guns before the zero hour, owing to the rigid instructions with regard to secrecy.

The Battery remained silent awaiting the bursting of the storm.

At zero hour on the morning of the 20th November, the Battery joined in the great general bombardment which opened on a front of several miles in support of the big attack on Cambrai, and continued for some hours until eventually, at 10 a.m., the rapid advance of our tanks, followed closely by the infantry, drove the enemy beyond the range of our guns.

The next day the Battery moved to a position further north, but on the same front on which the battle was proceeding, the change to open warfare and the general condition of the roads necessitating the employment of horse transport for the first and only time in the history of the Battery, and on the night of the 22nd, the guns were pulled into position in a dip in the open country between Demicourt and Doignies. This position was in many ways unique, as Bourlon Wood could be clearly seen in the distance and many of the Battery's targets were visible from the guns. The intense cold and absence of accommodation—the village of Doignies being merely a ruin—made living conditions severe, the majority of the personnel having to find cover under canvas or hastily constructed shelters.

On the 23rd November, various minor operations were undertaken on Moeuvres, Inchy and Bourlon Wood. The enemy counter-attacked in force on the 30th and captured Gouzeaucourt amongst other places, but failed to advance on the salient in front of the Battery. Wave after wave of enemy infantry, seen debouching from Bourlon Wood in massed formation, were caught by our fire and the losses suffered must have been enormous. On this and subsequent days, fierce fighting was

"Frezenberg Ridge," Ypres Battle, 1917

maintained, the Battery firing in one day alone as many as fifteen hundred shells.

Difficulties were increased at this time by the frequent transfer of batteries from one Artillery Group to another, necessitating the laying down of long lines of communication.

During the Cambrai battle communication with Group Headquarters was interrupted for a considerable time, leaving a great deal to the initiative of Major Fitzpatrick, commanding the Battery, who, especially during the counter-attack on the 30th, used his discretion in engaging targets which could be clearly seen from the battery position, varying the rate of fire according to the ammunition available at the guns.

Ammunition was sent up by light line to places in the vicinity and arrangements had to be made with other units for the provision of horse transport, while loading parties had to go out at night from the battery to find the ammunition, meet the general service wagons and load them up. Confusion resulted sometimes owing to change in rail-head dumps, and on more than one occasion it became necessary to load up six-inch ammunition wherever found in order to maintain the necessary dumps at the battery, while in one instance, in consequence of the bad condition of the roads, two hundred rounds of ammunition were brought up from the rail-head in two tanks.

There followed a few days in which the work of the Battery was largely confined to neutralising fire on hostile batteries and harassing important parts of the enemy lines. It is noteworthy that gas shells were first used by the Battery at this position, a large number of lachrymatory shells being fired into Bourlon Wood; prior to that 6-inch batteries had not been issued with this class of projectile, gas bombardments having been carried out with guns of a smaller calibre.

On the 5th December the British front was withdrawn, leaving the Battery in an open position within 1,400 yards of the enemy line, which was visible from No. 3 gun-pit.

Hostile shelling became increasingly active on Doignies, in which two other siege batteries had positions, and on the 3rd and 5th of December casualties were sustained at the billets, five men being killed and nine wounded, and, in consequence, the billets were removed to Beaumetz-les-Cambrai on the 7th, which, however, did not secure immunity from harassing fire. Lieutenant H. J. Henderson and a number of other ranks were gassed at Doignies.

On the 14th, at Beaumetz, while Major Fitzpatrick and Lieutenant P. D. Waller were making arrangements for the latter's transport to rail-head to proceed to England on leave, both were hit by a chance shell. The Major was instantly killed and Lieutenant Waller so seriously wounded that he died shortly afterwards. Gunner H. Summers was awarded the Meritorious Service Medal for his prompt assistance on this occasion, rendered at considerable personal risk. The loss of these two officers was keenly felt in the Battery, both being exceedingly popular, and the latter having served in the Battery prior to his promotion to commissioned rank.

The next senior officer, Lieutenant A. W. F. Roper, was left in charge of the Battery until Major Hall, Royal Garrison Artillery, arrived and took over command on the 18th. Lieutenant Roper was subsequently awarded the Military Cross for the able manner in which he carried out his duties under exceptionally trying circumstances, the two next senior officers being away at the time, while the strength of the Battery had again been very much reduced by casualties and sickness.

Second-Lieutenants H. C. M. Ross, Royal Garrison Artillery, N. E. Barrie and R. J. W. Charlton joined the Battery at Doignies, and Second-Lieutenant E. Hancock, Royal Garrison Artillery, at Beaumetz-les-Cambrai.

On the 18th the guns were pulled back into a position in front of Beaumetz, but no firing was done from this position, and on Christmas Eve, in pursuance of an order to proceed to the First Corps with a view to joining the 73rd and 125th (South African) Siege Batteries and the formation of a South African Brigade, the Battery went back to Grevillers, where its transport column was then parked. This change was in accordance with the general reorganisation of Heavy and Siege Artillery into permanent Brigades, and the opportunity thus afforded of collecting three South African Batteries into the same Brigade procured an identity for the South African Heavy Artillery which had long been the aim of all those interested in the Regiment, besides facilitating the reunion of friends in the various batteries who had not seen each other since coming to France.

On Christmas Day, in cold frosty weather, Arras was reached. A heavy fall of snow that evening gave a wintry setting to the scene, but although individuals were able to purchase some Christmas fare in the well-stocked shops in the town, a general feeling of disappointment was experienced that it had not been possible to carry out the programme of festivities, including a trip to Amiens, which had been arranged prior to the receipt of movement orders.

A two days' halt at Annezin on the outskirts of Bethune afforded opportunities of revisiting the latter town, which at that time had been very little damaged by shell-fire.

On the 29th December a move was made into position, the right section of the Battery going to La Bourse, while the left went to Beuvry, on the La Bassée sector of the front lying between Bethune and Lens. Here, for the first time, billets were found in houses and villages undamaged by shell-fire, whose inhabitants appeared to follow their normal occupations as though no war was raging and who were apparently indifferent to the fact that they were living within range of enemy guns. Coal-mines continued in full swing, and children passed to and fro daily on their way to school. The gunners now found it possible to vary the army diet by purchasing eggs, potatoes, and even pork chops, while light wines and French beer were also obtainable, and in every way the conditions of life improved vastly. The conditions obtaining were probably due to the line on this sector of the front having remained stationary since the battle of Neuve Chappelle in 1915, and no operations of any importance having taken place in the interim.

Both battery positions were reserve ones and particularly good, and it was the intention that the section at La Bourse should be a silent one.

The guns at Beuvry were registered on the 1st January, 1918, and thereafter became silent, while the section at La Bourse was suddenly called upon on the 4th January to answer an "S.O.S." call, although it had not been possible to register the line or the shooting of the guns.

Owing to the distance from the front line, enemy trenches were practically the only targets within range, and as the front was very quiet, very few targets were engaged, nor was there any sign of activity on the part of hostile artillery. On the 9th January, in pursuance of orders, the Battery went out on rest, leaving the guns in position at Beuvry in charge of a guard, while those from La Bourse accompanied the Battery for training purposes.

The whole of the 44th South African Brigade was billeted during the rest period in the vicinity of Manqueville, reached by way of Bethune and Lillers, and this was the first occasion on which entire brigades of Royal Garrison Artillery were brought out on rest. Opportunity was thus given for training and recreation, and football matches between the 71st, 73rd and 125th Siege Batteries were arranged and thoroughly enjoyed by all.

Major Brydon, formerly in command of the 73rd Siege Battery, on his return from hospital in England, took over the command of the

Battery from Major Hall during the stay at Manqueville, and Captain R. H. M. Hands, Second-Lieutenant H. Hall and Second-Lieutenant W. Drummond also joined the Battery from England. Battery Sergeant-Major Dacombe left for England on leave, and, owing to illness, did not return, and for a considerable period Quartermaster-Sergeant Wardrop acted in his place. Bombardier I. Isherwood was appointed Acting Battery Quartermaster.

The South African Batteries were inspected at Manqueville by Lieutenant-General Horne, commanding the First Army, in which the Battery was now serving, and photographs were taken of the personnel of each battery. Late in the month of January Lieutenant-General Smuts also reviewed the South African Batteries, this being the first occasion on which the South African Heavy Artillery Regiment was inspected by a South African Representative. The Hon. H. Burton, M.L.A., also arranged to visit the Brigade subsequently in July, but was prevented by illness at the last moment from doing so.

The apparent lack of interest in the batteries of the South African Heavy Artillery on the part of many eminent South Africans had hitherto been keenly felt by members of the unit.

After this rest, which was fully appreciated by all ranks, a return to the Line was made on the 30th January, the left section returning to Beuvry, while the right section relieved the personnel of the 237th Siege Battery in position at Locon, while the latter went on rest, returning eventually towards the end of February to its original position in La Bourse.

These were very quiet days, and beyond a little counter-battery work by the right section at Locon, practically no shooting was done.

Major Brydon and Capt. R. H. M. Hands, having come to France originally with the 73rd Siege Battery, were anxious to get back to the battery with which they had been so closely associated, and were now allowed to transfer; Major E. H. Tamplin and Captain J. R. McCarthy came to the 71st from the 73rd in their stead on the 14th February, 1918.

In pursuance of the general policy, adopted towards the end of 1917, of increasing the establishment of Siege Batteries from four to six guns, the 496th (South African) Siege Battery, which had been training in England for some months was brought out to France fully equipped, one-half of the Battery being posted to the 71st while the other went to the 73rd Siege Battery. Lieutenant Rutherford, the officer in charge of the section, was posted to the 71st. Major Tamplin decided to intermingle the personnel of the new section with that of the other two sections of the Battery. The two new guns were pulled into positions adjoining the left section at Beuvry.

The front became more active during March, but the work of the Battery was confined to supporting the 55th Division in raids into the enemy lines, and putting up a counter-barrage on the occasions of hostile raids into our lines. From the 12th March onwards until the 18th a marked increase in the activity of hostile batteries became noticeable.

The personnel of the Battery was now at full strength and the men were all very fit and keen, ready for the hard work which was expected with the advent of spring.

Major Tamplin assumed temporary command of the 44th South African Brigade, during the absence of Lieut.-Colonel Blew, D.S.O., leaving Capt. McCarthy in charge of the Battery. The Major was subsequently, on the 17th April, attached to the 55th Divisional Artillery in accordance with the new scheme of attaching senior gunner officers to divisions to maintain liaison and ensure effective co-operation.

Second-Lieutenant H. Hall, who had accepted a permanent commission in the Indian Cavalry, and Second Lieutenant W. J. Davies who had been posted to an Imperial Battery, left from the Beuvry position, while Quartermaster-Sergeant G. H. Miles came to the 71st from the 125th Siege Battery on the 9th April to fill the post of Battery Sergeant-Major.

The work of the Battery was now daily increasing, the advanced gun positions of the enemy being actively engaged, and on the 20th March our positions were heavily shelled prior to the heavy attack launched by the enemy on the Somme front on the morning of the 21st. On this occasion the enemy barrage was of unprecedented depth actually reaching the Battery position which was some 7,000 yards behind our front line. The barrage consisted of an ingenious mixture of high explosive and gas shell, rendering it exceedingly difficult to immediately detect the presence of the latter, the unmistakable burst of which was lost in the detonation of the high explosive.

Heavy shelling was maintained day after day, and on the 9th April a big attack was launched by the enemy on a wide front extending from north of Armentiers southwards to Givenchy, in front of the Battery position, where the attack was held.

We had only one casualty in the Battery, but on our left the enemy gained considerable ground, and other batteries in the Brigade suffered heavily, in consequence of which the guns at Beuvry had to be switched round through an angle of 120 degrees from the normal line of fire to engage advancing troops and advanced hostile batteries, firing at a much shorter range than had hitherto been possible from that position.

The 73rd (South African) Siege Battery in position on our left suffered very heavy casualties on the 9th April and ensuing days, no less than eight officers being killed or wounded, and in consequence Lieutenant Roper was seconded to that battery and assumed command temporarily. Captain McCarthy and Lieutenant Rutherford were subsequently transferred from the 71st to the 73rd Siege Battery, and Lieutenant Roper returned to the 71st on the 18th April.

The 9th of April also marked the commencement of a period of activity for the hitherto silent section at La Bourse, and in the next few days the six guns were almost continuously in action, and the strain of keeping the guns going and off-loading ammunition was increased by the frequent necessity for pulling out to engage fresh targets. It was a not uncommon occurrence for the various guns to be engaging different targets at the same time.

A further hostile attack was made on the 12th April on our immediate front, but was repulsed with a loss to the enemy of 750 prisoners on the 55th Divisional front alone. Targets at this time comprised chiefly active hostile batteries, transport columns on roads, which were reported to be packed with traffic, while aeroplane scouts were continually reporting fleeting opportunities of engaging moving targets.

It subsequently transpired, from photographs and other sources, that a great amount of destruction to enemy personnel and transport was effected. On one occasion the Battery fired on a hostile kite balloon which had been brought up to an advanced position behind the enemy line and was about to ascend.

On the 13th April, as a result of casualties from hostile shelling, and in pursuance of orders from the French authorities, the civilians still residing in the vicinity commenced to evacuate their homes, and many a pathetic sight was seen of whole families starting out, with such few belongings and household gods as they could manage to move with the very limited transport at their disposal, which frequently consisted of nothing better than a broken-down wheel-barrow. This evacuation was hastened on the 14th, when a hostile battery of 38 c.m. (15 inch) howitzers opened up on the village of Beuvry, causing considerable consternation, damage to property and some loss of life among the civil inhabitants. These super-heavies burst with terrific

A reinforced-concrete gun pit destroyed by our shell fire.   Wingles, La Bassée Sector.   May, 1918

force, and a large portion of the base of one shell—a piece weighing from 40 to 50 lbs.—fell in front of the Battery position nearly 1,000 yards from the spot where the shell burst.

At this time the roads behind the enemy lines were observed to be full of traffic, and on the 16th the front became so remarkably quiet that an uneasy feeling of impending attack was engendered. On the previous evening, aided by a brilliant moon and a cloudless sky, an enemy aeroplane descended to a low altitude over the position at Beuvry and hovered around for a long time, using its machine gun persistently. The Lewis gunner at the battery position opened fire on the aeroplane, which flew off and did not return.

At 4.30 a.m. on the 18th April, amid a very inferno of hostile shells, an S.O.S. was received to repel an attack launched in force against Givenchy, which was supported by an extremely heavy barrage of gas and high explosive shell of every calibre, and covering an area extending well behind the battery positions at Beuvry and La Bourse. The intensity of this barrage was without parallel in the memory of even the oldest members of the Battery. Throughout this period the Battery continued in action, with the exception of one gun which, owing to a sudden rise of water in the canal resulting in the flooding of the adjacent ground, it was impossible to fire until later in the day after it had been extricated with considerable difficulty.

The communications at Beuvry between the battery position, Brigade Headquarters and the various forward observation posts were greatly facilitated by an elaborate system of buried cables which had been in operation for some time, and although all lines were badly cut during the bombardment, re-establishment of communication was not a difficult matter. It was, however, a heavy day for the signallers owing to the persistency of intense shelling, and all of them were kept fully employed throughout the day. The signals staff deserve recognition for their continued efforts to maintain communications frequently under circumstances involving considerable risk.

The Battery was, notwithstanding, out of all touch with Brigade Headquarters and the front line for a time during a most critical period, and the officer on duty at Beuvry, Second-Lieutenant E. Hancock, was forced to rely entirely on his own judgment. He was subsequently awarded the Military Cross for the very able manner in which he handled the situation and kept the Battery in action under extremely trying circumstances, engaging fresh targets according to the intensity and direction of the hostile bombardment. The enemy bombardment slackened towards mid-day, but about that time the enemy appeared to be registering on the battery position with aircraft observation, and succeeded in setting light to some of the ammunition, but shelling ceased shortly afterwards.

The day was in many respects a remarkable one; no one was killed, only eight men were wounded at Beuvry and three at La Bourse, while in the billets no one was injured, notwithstanding that more than one of the houses used were destroyed, and one cellar, sheltering some dozen men, was blown in. In addition to the above casualties twenty-seven men subsequently suffered from the effects of gas.

The attack on Givenchy was successfully beaten back with great loss to the enemy, and the portion of the front covered by the 44th South African Brigade remained intact, with the exception of a couple of outposts subsequently recaptured in counter-attacks. On the following night the Battery supported a successful counter-attack by the 55th Division on Route "A" Keep and Piccadilly Trench, strong points which constantly changed hands during the ensuing days, and were the scenes of very bitter fighting.

By this time the position at Beuvry had lost much of its value owing to the loss of ground north-east of Bethune, and arrangements were consequently made to remove the Battery to a less exposed position behind the village of Beuvry. During the movement an S.O.S. was received, necessitating the pulling of one gun back into position, as in these critical days it was essential to get every gun possible into action in reply to such calls. Three guns fired from the old position and one from the new, and after the counter-attack had been successfully met, the transfer thus interrupted was finally effected, but was of a fleeting nature. Only two guns fired from the new position, and on the 21st April it was decided to concentrate all six guns at the La Bourse position. Two guns were, however, again detached the following day, and placed in a position adjoining the Beuvry Cemetery, but were withdrawn from there at the end of the month, as hostile batteries concentrated on the position whenever the guns opened fire.

The end of April saw the close of what was probably one of the most strenuous periods the Battery had ever experienced, no less than 17,431 rounds being fired between the 9th April and the 30th April, while the two guns at La Bourse disposed of 950 rounds between 4.30 a.m. and 11 p.m. on the 18th April.

The record of this period cannot be closed without a tribute to the excellent work of Staff-Sergeant Artificer Hopkins and his assistants, who by careful and constant attention were instrumental in keeping all six guns in action during this time, and by intelligent anticipation avoided minor defects and mishaps, which might have necessitated the sending of one or more guns to workshops.

The casualties during March and April were remarkably few considering the circumstances, and amounted to fifteen, excluding the gas cases already mentioned, which for the most part were not serious.

Second-Lieutenant M. E. Wright, Royal Garrison Artillery, and Second-Lieutenant D. Culverwell arrived and were taken on the strength of the Battery, from the 21st and 28th April respectively.

A scheme of rear billets was now adopted in order to prevent unnecessary casualties, and off-duty crews were housed for a time at Verquigneul, but a week later, owing to the latter village being subjected to harassing fire at night, fresh billets were found in Ruitz, some kilometres behind the line, where shacks were erected in a wood, and from there relief crews were taken up to the battery position in motor lorries.

On the 1st May, 1918, all six guns were again in the original position at La Bourse, but in view of the activity of hostile artillery a further move was made to a new position some 200 yards in rear, while two guns were sent up to occupy a forward position at Annequin, for the specific purpose of destructive shoots, with aeroplane observation, on a hostile battery and an ammunition dump, which tasks were eventually effected on the 9th May, bad weather having prevented earlier completion. A further object in moving one section of the Battery up into a forward position was the idea of misleading the enemy as to the actual strength of artillery on the particular front. On the 10th May the six guns were again concentrated at La Bourse, but, beyond a little counter-battery work and harassing fire at night, there was not much to do.

It was thought at this time that the enemy was preparing for another attack, and on the 25th May, 1918, two guns were again sent forward to Annequin to get within range of hostile batteries for purposes of destructive shoots.

This new position after two days came under heavy fire from the enemy and four men were wounded. Second-Lieutenant D. Culverwell was awarded the Military Cross, and Corporal W. J. Davis, Signallers S. C. A. Cosser and A. Ellis the Military Medal for the excellent work performed at this position under very trying circumstances. Corporal

Davis rendered conspicuous service in attending to wounded under shell-fire, and Signallers Cosser and Ellis were frequently engaged in repairing telephone lines under heavy shell-fire.

Another move of the forward section was then made in order to avoid further casualties, and eventually this section settled down in a position behind Fosse 9 at Annequin, and a considerable amount of good work was done from there, one and occasionally two destructive shoots on hostile batteries being undertaken daily, whenever weather conditions were suitable for aerial observation.

Hostile artillery continued in activity and the section at La Bourse suffered twenty casualties on the 25th May from a gas bombardment, necessitating a further alteration in the position of the gun-pits. The fact that the line on this sector of the front had been practically stationary for over three years, and all our old gun positions had been recorded by the enemy, rendering it increasingly difficult to select new suitable battery positions and side-stepping positions, more especially as the flat nature of the country and the comparative absence of trees reduced positions from which gun flashes could be concealed from the enemy to a minimum.

Second-Lieutenants J. V. Brade and S. B. Gwillam joined the Battery from England, but the latter was shortly afterwards attached to the First Corps Artillery School as an Instructor. Sergeant H. W. Meacham was transferred from the 75th (South African) Siege Battery to fill the post of Quartermaster-Sergeant in place of Quartermaster-Sergeant J. W. Wardrop, evacuated on account of illness. Second-Lieutenant F. W. Mellish was transferred in June from the 73rd Siege Battery to the 71st.

On the 1st June the 55th Division made a request for a liaison officer to carry out several important shoots on nests of machine guns and fortified strong points in the enemy line, and the battery was placed at the disposal of the Division, Lieutenant Green being temporarily attached to the Infantry Brigade. Several successful shoots were carried out by the guns at La Bourse on these points, although observation was difficult to obtain. Lieutenant A. P. Green was awarded the Military Cross for his services as forward observation officer on this occasion.

On the 28th June the whole battery was pulled out into a reserve position at Houchin, and during the ensuing period of rest the time was occupied in training gun-layers, lectures on map-reading, and other subjects.

A lot of time was also devoted to training for the Brigade Sports, which were attended by Lieutenant-General Holland, in command of the 1st Corps. They were held on the 18th July, and the 71st Siege Battery was very successful, winning the tug-of-war and a number of other events. The shooting competitions were held some days later when the Battery again met with some measure of success although it did not gain the premier place. On the 17th July a very interesting lecture was delivered by Colonel Gordon of the Royal Scots Fusiliers, on "Causes and effects of the War."

On the 26th July a number of officers and men journeyed South to the outskirts of Arras, where the other South African Brigade (50th) was in position, and a most enjoyable day resulted. A cricket match and a tug-of-war took place between the 74th and 71st Batteries, in which the laurels were won by the former.

The Battery returned to the line on the 31st July, one section occupying a silent position in front of Sailly-la-Bourse, and four guns going into action in the village of Vermelles, to the north-west of Loos, and the scene of very heavy fighting in 1914 and 1915, as a result of which hardly a wall had been left standing in the village.

Billets were at first found in Le Brebis, but more comfortable ones were subsequently found at Coupigny, on the outskirts of Hersin, on the 8th August. A considerable amount of work was done from the Vermelles position, and an average of 300 rounds was fired daily in destructive shoots on hostile batteries, if the weather was sufficiently clear to admit of aeroplane observation, while wire-cutting tasks and gas bombardments were also carried out. The Battery position was shelled on the 3rd August and thereafter was frequently subjected to hostile shelling, and, as a result of a particularly heavy gas bombardment on 6th September, Second-Lieutenant E. Hancock and seventeen other ranks left the Battery suffering from the effects of gas.

The two guns at Sailly-la-Bourse were withdrawn from that position after some weeks and transferred to a position in a sunken road just outside the village of Mazingarbe for a few days, but were soon afterwards brought up into a position on the left of the four guns at Vermelles, which had been moved into new positions some little distance from the original position shelled so heavily on the 6th September.

Quartermaster-Sergeant C. G. Duffy of the 73rd (South African) Siege Battery was appointed Battery Sergeant-Major of the 71st Siege Battery, *vice* Battery Sergeant-Major G. H. Miles, who had been granted a commission in the Royal Garrison Artillery.

Meanwhile, enemy high velocity guns had been increasingly active on towns in rear of the line, and a number of soldiers and civilians were killed and injured one night at Coupigny when the village was heavily shelled. Only one casualty occurred at the billets at this time, but it was considered desirable to return to the former billets in the wood at Ruitz to avoid the possibility of unnecessary casualties.

The front became quieter for a time as no operation by the enemy on anything like a large scale was anticipated, but the initiative was now gradually being assumed by our infantry, and a considerable amount of work was done by the Battery in support of operations by the 11th Division, resulting in the capture of Fosse 8, "The Craters," and the Railway Triangle south-west of La Bassée. Captain Roper was attached to the 11th Division as liaison officer for a period of three weeks from the 1st August.

Early in September the billets were again removed from the wood at Ruitz, and the old position at the sunken road at Mazingarbe was occupied and used as living quarters for the personnel, existing dug-outs being utilised, and additional shacks were also erected.

A feature of the last few days at Vermelles was the large number of instances in which the fire of practically all the batteries in the Corps was concentrated at appointed times, for periods of five minutes at intense rates of fire, on various important strong points in the enemy's lines, the effect of which must have been appalling.

A particularly noteworthy task was the destruction of wire in front of La Bassée, owing to the great difficulty of obtaining a suitable post of observation. An attempt was at first made to carry out the shoot by means of visual signalling from the top of Fosse 8, which, however, proved unsatisfactory owing to the impossibility of communicating with the forward observation officer by similar methods as they would have been observed by the enemy. Special telephone lines were consequently laid down the same night and the shoot successfully completed the following day.

Meanwhile, reconnaissances were made of forward positions in preparation for the support of any attack that might be decided on.

On the nights of the 29th and the 30th September very heavy concentrations of fire with gas shell were made on the villages of Douvrin, Wingles, Haines, Hantay, Berclau and Salomé with a view to harassing the enemy's retirement which appeared to be then in progress. On the 1st October, 1918 it became apparent that a general withdrawal to the line of the Canal de la Haute Deule was in progress and preparations were immediately made for a forward move. Three guns were taken forward at dusk to a position at the Bois de la Haye; on the ridge a few hundred yards behind our old front

An enemy gun position after "destructive" shoot by our "heavies"
Douvrin, La Bassée Sector. July, 1918

line, went into action the next day and continued to harass the enemy troops and transport. This was, however, only a temporary position and the other three guns, after working parties had been out all night filling in shell holes to render the road passable, were taken forward over the area which had hitherto been "No Man's Land" into Hulluch: a journey of some 3,000 yards, occupying nine hours.

These guns were the first to cross the old front lines into evacuated enemy territory, and by going at once into action were able to perform a good deal of very useful work. The three guns left behind at the Bois de la Haye were brought up into a position adjoining the three forward guns in Hulluch on the 6th October, 1918, and the road having been vastly improved in the meantime, these guns were only out of action for two and a-half hours during the operation. Very great difficulties had to be surmounted during these moves, owing to the condition of the road through the old front lines, which had suffered from constant shelling. The main Vermelles-Hulluch road was the only one available at this point for all classes of transport or troops going forward or returning, and was very frequently subjected to concentrations of fire from hostile batteries, with the result that traffic was frequently held up. The presence of two huge mine craters at the cross roads in Hulluch also added to the many difficulties. Ammunition was at first brought up to the new position in general service wagons, but after two days the motor lorry drivers, exercising great care and ingenuity to avoid getting ditched, succeeded in bringing the lorries up to the position, although their task was by no means easy, for there was no moon nor was it possible to show any lights.

During the following days the Battery was heavily engaged principally in answering calls from the air-scouts who were constantly reporting the positions of hostile batteries in action or movement of enemy infantry or motor transport. Gas bombardments and destructive shoots on machine gun nests were also carried out.

Two days after the difficult move into Hulluch had been carried out, orders were received for two guns to be sent back with complete personnel to the First Corps Artillery School at Herly for demonstration purposes.

In preparation for the immediate following-up of any further withdrawal by the enemy, rear billets were, for the time, abolished, and the personnel lived at the battery position.

On the 15th the enemy continued the withdrawal, and our infantry effected a crossing of the Haute Deule Canal, while the Battery was continuously engaged in protecting them by neutralising hostile batteries in conjunction with aeroplane observation, on one occasion no less than twenty-three calls being answered by the Battery in a period of one and a-half hours.

The same evening, at 7.30 p.m., two guns were pulled out and went into position on the canal bank opposite Meurchin, being ready for action at 11.30 p.m.

The Battery was not destined to fire for several days as the enemy was now in full retreat. As soon as a pontoon bridge had been thrown across the canal and had been pronounced available for heavy traffic, these two guns went forward on the morning of the 17th into Carvin, being the first siege guns of the Corps to cross the Canal. These guns were taken through Carvin and on to Libercourt, which was reached about noon. The enemy had, however, retired entirely out of range of siege artillery, and a return was therefore made to Carvin until the following day when an advance was made as far as Jonquerie, some ten kilometres further east.

A reconnaissance party of an officer and two signallers had the somewhat embarrassing experience of being the first British troops to enter the village of Mons-et-Pevele after its evacuation by the Germans, and received a very hearty ovation from the civilian population which was overjoyed at its release from the restraint suffered during the enemy occupation.

The remaining two guns from Hulluch joined the forward section on the 20th, after encountering considerable difficulties owing to the ditching of lorries. All problems of transport of guns, stores, and personnel at this time, were rendered most acute by the systematic and thorough manner in which the German engineers had blown up bridges and mined every cross-road. The energy displayed by Lieutenant H. T. Watts, Army Service Corps, the officer in charge of the column of motor transport attached to the Battery, and the indefatigable manner in which, during the period of seven days occupied by the move to Lesdain, the men under his command worked to get the guns forward, are here appreciatively recorded. Their handling of these transport problems was largely instrumental at all times in getting the guns promptly into action. The way in which the guns and limbers were hauled off hard roads by the "Four-Wheeled Drives" right into the positions they were to occupy, thereby saving both time and the strain on the personnel of the Battery occasioned by man-handling heavy guns over rough ground reflected great credit on the capability and resource of the drivers.

36

On the 23rd October, the two remaining sections of the Battery moved forward to Genech and from there, on the 26th, went into position in the vicinity of Lesdain, some 2,700 yards west of the Escaut Canal, where the third section joined the Battery from Herly on the 3rd November. The Battery was now in fairly well wooded rolling country, but considerable difficulty was still experienced in selecting suitable gun positions from which flashes could be concealed from the enemy, who held the line of the canal. A good deal of counter-battery and other work was carried out from the two positions here. Hostile batteries were exceedingly active, distributing, throughout the day and night, sudden bursts of fire over the area occupied by the Brigade.

This activity was especially marked on the two days preceding the further withdrawal of the enemy on the night of the 7th November, and it was at dawn on the following morning that the Battery fired its last salvo in the war. Owing to the impossibility of crossing the canal with heavy guns until adequate pontoon bridges had been constructed, the Battery was unable to follow the enemy in his hasty retreat immediately preceding the conclusion of the armistice.

On the morning of the 9th a Brigade reconnaissance party, including one officer and two other ranks from the Battery, set out to keep in touch with the advanced screens of infantry, with a view to selecting new battery positions. The party advanced through Callenelle and continued on until about 2 o'clock, when the presence of strong enemy patrols in adjoining villages was reported. By this time a distance of some 21,000 yards from the Battery position had been covered, and the party was practically half way towards the historic town of Mons, and well in advance of the infantry. In view of the presence of hostile patrols and as the enemy was still in full retreat it became necessary to turn back without selecting battery positions. The people living in the villages through which the party passed were at first a little suspicious and reluctant to furnish information, but as soon as they were convinced that the uniform was British and realised that British troops were advancing, expressed their joy and even offered to share their meagre supplies of food with the members of the party, and hastened to unearth secret stores of excellent wine, buried prior to the German occupation.

During the last ten months of the war, and especially at Beuvry and La Bourse in April, at Vermelles in August, and later at Hulluch and Lesdain, the Battery was subjected to heavy shelling by the enemy, and it is an extraordinary fact that during that period no one was killed, while very few casualties of a really serious nature occurred, an amazing run of good fortune upon which the Battery might well congratulate itself. A fact which makes this good fortune the more surprising was the subsequent discovery from maps found in German dug-outs, that almost every position occupied by the Battery in the La Bassée sector was, sooner or later, accurately located by the enemy.

Various decorations awarded to members of the Battery, numbering sixteen in all, have already been mentioned, and in addition Sergeant H. Mann was awarded the coveted French Medaille Militaire and also received the Meritorious Service Medal for his able services during the long period he was with the Battery. Lieutenant F. W. Mellish was mentioned in despatches for his services in the closing stages of the campaign.

The total casualties during the period of over two and a-half years in France and Belgium reached the figure of two hundred and seventy-seven, which included twenty-six deaths.' A large number of the casualties was the result of gas bombardments, and in many of these cases recovery was merely a matter of rest and treatment. Only one death from sickness occurred during the Battery's stay with the British Expeditionary Force abroad, a period of nearly three years.

This brief history should not be concluded without a tribute to the French civilian population with whom the Battery was in constant touch during the closing stages of the war. Their industry and quiet determination, the apparent stoical indifference exhibited by them in the face of danger and even of death, and their capacity for calmly carrying on as usual, even under shell fire, was a constant source of wonder and admiration to the members of the Battery. In the summer, old men, bent of back, might be seen working in the fields as late as eight or nine o'clock at night, while later as the harvest ripened, it was not uncommon to see aged men and women gathering in the corn in front of our forward positions, some 3,000 yards from the front line. In Noeux-les-Mines, which at one time was daily subjected to a heavy bombardment by hostile batteries of high velocity guns, and bombed almost continually night after night, one would see old women calmly sweeping up the broken glass and the men optimistically fixing new tiles on the roofs. Tiny children of four or five would all be playing a useful part in the work of the house while their mothers were working in the fields.

71st (S.A.) Siege Battery.　"Carvin," November, 1918

Reminiscences.

Sz-z-z-upp! Sz-z-z-upp! Sz-z-z-upp! Sz-z-z-upp! "By Jove! those were close. Get out quick before the next salvo." "Ikona! we're as safe here as anywhere." "———— it! I have come out without my pants." "And I've left my tin hat behind." Why on earth any one wants any reminiscences of France, I can't think. I only want to forget it all *toute de suite.* Just imagine any one retaining pleasant recollections of "All Guns action!" at 04.00 on a winter's morning, with all that it means—groping, half awake, for hand-spikes; falling over cartridge boxes on a pitch black night; stumbling into shell-holes on the way to the night picket; barking your shins on the trail, and brushing frozen snow off a stack of shells. Or who would willingly remember an ammunition fatigue on a cold frosty night when, in an endeavour to get up a three-feet bank you come to grief, drop the shell on your pet corn, and then, to cap it all, hear the voice of authority coming out of the inky darkness: "What the ———— are you doing? You can't dump those here."

On second thoughts, however, I think we have all established some fast friendships which, forged in the furnace of hard times endured together, will endure for a lifetime; and we will gladly cherish some memories of our stay on the Western Front, while many an incident will conjure up a smile in the distant future.

There is the incident of the A.S.C. Major at Mailly-Maillet, fearfully keen on helping to win the War, who got permission to pull the lanyard. He was carefully coached, but we forgot to give him some cotton wool, and the gun-pits were on the small side. "Stand By!" came, and he stood expectant, nerves all taut. "Fire!" Off blew his cap and it took him all his time to keep his feet, and he looked very relieved when he was assured that his anatomy was still complete. The breech was opened, and he bent down and looked up the flaming bore. "It is all right, Sir! it's gone," came in the quiet tones of the layer.

It was, I think, at Bazentin that one of the signallers was out on the lines and got strafed pretty badly, getting slightly wounded. He simply couldn't raise a buzz, and when even his patience was exhausted, he went back, chucked down his "Don 3" and asked "Mac" to fix it up; and it was only then that the latter found half of it had been blown away.

The scene was Ypres and shelling had been fast and furious, and an

39

O.K. had just been registered on our canteen, then under the capable management of our cheery friend Ike, who was busily employed in fishing his stock out of the débris. A few minutes later in walked "Toc Ac" for some cigarettes. "Well, my boy," says Ike, "we're rather busy just now, you'd better come back to-morrow." A little later some one else: "Any fruit, Ike?" "There you are, my lad." "But it's got a hole in it." "Yes, you see that is damaged by shell-fire and would be a franc to anybody else, but we'll only charge you 75."

There was the somewhat unpleasant experience of the officer who was out on O.P. duty at Ervillers with two signallers, and was arrested by an Infantry Patrol who suspected them of cutting telephone wires. It was with difficulty that they satisfied Battalion Headquarters of their bona fides, especially as Tommy had only the day before had a close crop. Then again the latter's bad half hour at Heytesbury House, when he lost his way while doing a caterpillar stunt on his hands and knees, and, with pip squeaks dropping all round him, got nearer to the enemy line than was healthy, is not an experience any one will envy him.

Many of us have had advice from officers both good, bad and indifferent, but nothing is likely to beat the "Bull Dog's" when he suggested to Bazentin Bill the best method to employ in developing his tenor voice.

"Rum Up!" two magic words that bring in their wake a score of recollections; of the many a slip 'twixt cup and lip at Doignies, and then again the cold night on the road midway between Gouzeaucourt and Doignies when, in the cold midnight hour, the voice of the S.M. led one like a will o' the wisp through the pitch black night, through ditches and barbed wire. Every one fell in for rum that night in more senses than one, and fell in again on the journey back. The ammunition fatigue at Heudicourt had the good fortune to strike a rum issue, and we wonder what the more temperate members, who preferred to add a little "water," thought. We also wonder whether it has ever since dawned on the rather youthful officer who joined us at ———, why his presence was so frequently required at the guns on nights when there had been a rum issue. In regard to rum we have often wondered whether all batteries are treated alike in the matter, as we could never understand why the 301st Siege, whom we relieved at Ypres, and the 237th who took over at Locon, should have complained that they didn't get the rum that we got.

Once started, old memories come back thick and fast. Never shall I forget the look on the face of the officer on duty in the B.C.'s post, tired after a heavy day, on receiving from a telephonist a message on the usual strip of paper, requesting him to carry out an early reconnaissance of "all the Battery positions in Europe" and his relief on learning subsequently that he was only expected to devote his attention to the "Battery positions in your Group," while "Jammy's" embarrassment at the affectionate reception accorded him by the ladies of Mons-la-Pevele was a treat for the gods.

We have fond recollections of Lucie, with her charm of manner and her extraordinary knowledge of English, of Madge's wonderful eyes, the excellence of Fideline's eggs and chips, and the extreme neatness of Julia's attire.

On the pathetic side there is the death of ——, Bob's little dog, always his best friend, never separated from him, until his master was sent down the line, and the poor wee thing never got over it. We recall with a smile the incident at Doignies when a certain N.C.O. fed up to the eyes with the monotony of trench warfare, made his way towards the front line, armed with a "walking wounded" notice board, and determined to challenge Jerry to mortal combat. The fact that his lethal weapon was somewhat cumbersome and the way long, prevented him from attaining his objective is mentioned in explanation of his cheery countenance being still among us.

Poor old George going west has left a blank in our ranks not easily filled; he was the source of many a jest; and his fund of dry humour, his imperturbable good nature, notwithstanding the incessant chaff to which he was subjected, endeared him to us all. It is a marvel to me how he escaped injury at Manqueville when, finding the billets somewhat cold, he put some wood into the Canadian stove we had and added a little petrol, apparently oblivious to the presence in the stove of a couple of part charges, but even that flare up failed to disturb his equanimity.

We forget for the moment the name of the No. 1. who, in an area where auxiliary Aiming Points were hard to find, selected a dug-out chimney, but can picture his consternation at finding on the following day, not only no chimney but no dug-out, and his chagrin on being informed that the infantry field kitchen had moved on. We rather fancy it was the same N.C.O. who on being gently rebuked by the O.C. on some matter, took the bull by the horns and, putting no his best smile, requested to be reduced to the rank of permanent mess orderly.

There was also the layer who confused the light in the officers' mess with his own night picket, and yet another, possibly a descendant of the ancient mariner, dispensed with night pickets altogether and laid his guns by the stars. At Lievin one of the guns was laid by the corner window of a broken-down house, but one night Jerry blew off the corner window in such a manner that the layer did not at first notice anything wrong, and cheerfully took the next one for his A.P.

Many minor incidents stand out clearly in one's mind, such as the roaring fire and spirit of conviviality in the early hours of Christmas morning at Grevillers (1917), the splendid Christmas dinner at Arras later in the day, the route marches and snow fights at Manqueville, the sick parades on alternate days at Beaumetz, the turn out of the guard at Beuvry, complete with muffler and "pull-through," the bathes at Ruitz, the night out in the open at Coupigny, and the 500 yards cross country run at Carvin, while occurrences at Barlin and Annezin are, curiously enough, shrouded in the mists of the past which unfortunately prevent elaboration.

A few of us will recollect the free bath at La Bourse, which some of us had while others didn't, and the total absence of logic displayed by the wee Scot in the course of ensuing arguments who wasted much of his somewhat odorous breath in heated expostulation.

It was at Doignies that Jerry was unpleasantly active in the afternoons and seemed to mark down the water fatigue for especial attention, particularly old Dad who, although he always came up with a broad smile, did not altogether relish the rôle of Aunt Sally.

Ammunition fatigues are hardly a fit subject for pleasant recollections, and the only man I can remember who would come up at the double and be the first on the scene on the call "Ammunition Up!" was old Busty when he joined us behind the Fosse at Annequin.

"Those *were* evenings!" a remark frequently heard in the precincts of the officers' mess, and many of us will often recall the various incidents with a silent chuckle. "Here you are, old man. Here's the planchette and there are the latest operation orders, this is the shoot we are doing and the line to Brigade is down. Well, Cheer-ho!" and without wasting any more time the officer going off duty disappeared into the night towards the Ypres billets, picking his road carefully to avoid any route likely to receive particular attention from Jerry's batteries.

How often we had to leave the Bavaria House position at a moment's notice to take refuge in the pill-box along the Decauville line, how many a meal was interrupted by crumps, and how we used to munch an improvised meal in the shelter of that self-same pill-box, although it was not often very much in the way of "skoff," that was collected in the stampede.

We would criticise Jerry's shooting from the comparative safety of our refuge as he pumped an assortment of 5.9's and 8-inch into the position.

"Cocky! there goes your kya," and "Oh—! There goes 'B' sub's shack." Later we would venture back all on the *qui vive* to leg it again on the slightest sign of Jerry opening up.

We can still picture in our mind the scene at Ypres, with a rum issue on. One N.C.O. had just drawn his and deputised for a few others when Jerry opened up and the queue rapidly dispersed. Our friend, however, got down to it in regulation fashion, but not before he had carefully placed his mug on the ground and covered it with his tin hat.

Then there was the cartridge member who had just "coom oop," who, on the command "3rd Charge Load!" was seen trying to cram three full charges into the breech : the layer who laid his gun by a blade of grass when he could no longer see his fog picket; and yet another, who, notwithstanding the brilliant brass "L" on his arm, was very worried because he couldn't level his cross-bubble with his elevating wheel.

And poor old absent-minded Jock at Becordel having to go out on lines very early in the day, sleeping in until the last moment and then hurrying off with his little bundle of skoff over his shoulder, which later in the day proved to be nothing more appetising than a bundle of washing. This recalls a somewhat similar incident at Doignies when kind-hearted old Dad trudged all the way from Beaumetz to the guns with a bag of biscuits he had made for the boys, who were rather ungrateful on finding his bag contained firewood.

Two members of the Battery will often laugh over the occasion when Jerry started shelling the sunken road at Doignies in the middle of the night. The instinct to clear, which we all feel, especially when newly arrived at the battery, prompted them to leave their comparatively safe dug-out, and they discussed the problem after every fresh salvo, and eventually—incidentally, after it was all over—they disappeared precipitately into the dark and sought the shelter of a limber, under which they spent the remaining hours in fitful slumber.

Another member of the Battery will always regret that we never got to close grips with the enemy, as he has never forgotten, or forgiven, the night at Ruitz when the constant earth tremors due to bombing dislodged from the shelf above his head an open tin of syrup, and he was awakened by a steady stream of sticky liquid trickling over his face.

We wonder whether Jim, Elsie and Frikkie still hold that a haystack is adequate protection from a 13-in. H. Vic.

We all enjoyed the Saturday afternoon in Aire and the Rugby match against the Army School, and particularly the hospitality of the Froggy who put up a barrel of beer for the occasion. It is a pity that difficulties of language prevented him from adequately conveying how he felt towards us all. We were all rather stony that day, and deputed Jim to ascertain whether one of the officers could make a noise like a ten-franc note. "Well, Corporal S——, I am awfully sorry, but I have only got about seven francs on me." "Well, sir, five would do!"

We hear—a rather lengthy process perhaps—that there is a ward in a certain hospital in England where they believe in the open-air cure and Union Jacks are much in evidence.

The cinematograph film that was taken at Beuvry of the scratch gun team in action, with Shorty and Midge ramming home, ought to be worth seeing if it is ever filmed in South Africa, as it should show not only how a gun is loaded and fired, but also how injuries are sometimes inflicted.

In glancing through the Battery history, I notice a reference to the light French wines. Whoever wrote that could not have been on the fatigue from La Bourse to Bethune—most of us found them particularly heavy after the first mile.

What will the inhabitants of Beuvry do with all the razors they will doubtless find buried in the ruins of old Seventy-one's billets?

At some future date, when we are all sitting down at the annual S.A.H.A. dinner that we hope will be held, certain faces will grow slightly pale when "La Bourse, 1918," is seen figuring in the wine list as a liqueur.

Napooh!

Sectors of the Battle Areas on the Western Front in which the 71st (South African) Siege Battery has been in action, showing the various battery positions occupied.

SOMME AREA.—Mailly-Maillet, 25th May, 1916.

BATTLE OF YPRES.—Ypres, 4th to 14th June, 1916.

BATTLE OF THE SOMME AND THE ANCRE.—Mailly-Maillet, 18th June, 1916; Becordel, 5th July, 1916; Bazentin, 20th September, 1916; Beauval (on rest), 22nd December, 1916; Ovillers, 2nd January, 1917.

ENEMY RETREAT FROM THE SOMME, AND BATTLES OF BULLECOURT.—Thiepval (2 guns), 8th March, 1917; Ervillers, 1 gun from 23rd March, 1917, 4 guns from 3rd April, 1917; Mory, 1st May, 1917; Croisilles, 4th July, 1917.

BATTLE OF YPRES.—Ypres, Menin Gate, 2 guns from 31st August, 1917, 4 guns from 15th September, 1917; Cavalry Farm, 28th September, 1917; Bavaria House, 8th October, 1917.

LENS SECTOR.—Lievin, 25th October, 1917.

BATTLE OF CAMBRAI.—Gouzeaucourt, 13th November, 1917; Doignies, 22nd November, 1917; Beaumetz-les-Cambrai, 18th December, 1917.

LA BASSEE SECTOR.—Beuvry (Left Section) and La Bourse (Right Section), 29th December, 1917; Manqueville (on rest), 9th January, 1918; Beuvry (Left Section) and Locon (Right Section), 30th January, 1918; La Bourse (Right Section), 25th February, 1918.

BATTLE OF THE LYS.—LA BASSÉE SECTOR.—Beuvry (4 guns) and La Bourse (2 guns), 6th March, 1918; Beuvry Slag-heap (2 guns), 20th April, 1918; La Bourse (6 guns), 21st April, 1918; Beuvry Cemetery (2 guns), 22nd April, 1918.

LA BASSÉE SECTOR.—La Bourse (6 guns), 1st May, 1918; Annequin (2 guns), 2nd to 9th May, 1918; Annequin (2 guns), 25th May, 1918; Houchin (Reserve position), 28th June, 1918; Vermelles (4 guns) and Sailly-la-Bourse (2 guns), 31st July, 1918; Mazingarbe (2 guns from Sailly), 2nd September, 1918; Vermelles (6 guns), 8th September, 1918.

GREAT ENEMY RETREAT.

First Withdrawal. — Bois-de-la-Haye (3 guns), 1st October, 1918; Hulluch (3 guns), 6th October, 1918; Hulluch (6 guns), 6th October, 1918; First Corps School, Herly (2 guns), 8th October, 1918; Canal Bank, opposite Meurchin (2 guns), 15th October, 1918.

Second Withdrawal.—Lesdain (4 guns), 26th October, 1918; Lesdain (6 guns), 3rd November, 1918.

Decorations.

B.S.M. S. G. Dacombe awarded the D.C.M. for services at Ypres in June, 1916.

Major H. C. Harrison awarded the D.S.O. for services at Pozières in July, 1916.

Corporal H. E. Robinson awarded the M.M. for services at Pozières in July, 1916.

Captain A. E. Rann awarded the M.C. for services at Bazentin in November, 1916.

Bombardier G. W. Munro awarded the M.M. for services at Bazentin in November, 1916.

Gunner J. M. Turnbull awarded the M.M. for services at Bazentin in November, 1916.

Gunner G. T. B. Tasker awarded the M.M. for services at Bazentin in November, 1916.

Corporal E. Naitby awarded the M.M. for services at Ypres in September, 1917.

Bombardier H. Summers awarded the M.S.M. for services at Beaumetz in December, 1917.

2nd-Lieut. E. Hancock awarded the M.C. for services at Beuvry on 18th April, 1918.

2nd-Lieut. D. Culverwell awarded the M.C. for services at Annequin in June, 1918.

Corporal Davis awarded the M.M. for services at Annequin in June, 1918.

Gunner S. C. A. Cosser awarded the M.M. for services at Annequin in June, 1918.

Gunner A. Ellis awarded the M.M. for services at Annequin in June, 1918.

Lieut. A. W. F. Roper awarded the M.C. for services at Doignies in December, 1917.

Lieut. A. P. Green awarded the M.C. for services rendered while Liaison Officer with the 55th Division in June, 1918.

Major E. H. Tamplin awarded the M.C. for services in G.S.W.A. Campaign.

Sergeant T. A. White awarded the M.S.M. for general services throughout.

Sergeant H. Mann awarded the French Medaille Militaire and Meritorious Service Medal for general services in the field.

Lieut. A. P. Green mentioned in despatches for services at Ypres.

Bombardier A. T. Petters mentioned in despatches for services at Ypres.

2nd-Lieut. F. W. Mellish mentioned in despatches for services rendered during the final stages of the Campaign.

Appointments.

Captain H. C. Harrison in command.

Capt. A. E. Rann.   2nd-Lt. E. Mason.
2nd-Lt. P. N. G. Fitzpatrick.   2nd-Lt. A. B. Crump.
S. G. Dacombe - Battery Sergeant-Major.
T. H. White   - Battery Quartermaster-Sergeant.

1st Jan., 1916.	Bombardier A. W. F. Roper promoted to 2nd-Lieutenant (74th S.B.)
1st Jan., 1916.	Bombardier E. A. Mitchell promoted to 2nd-Lieutenant (71st S.B.)
15th Apl., 1916.	Bombardier R. S. Miller promoted to 2nd-Lieutenant (125th S.B.)
18th June, 1916.	Lt. R. Levy (seconded from 44th Brigade).
1st Aug., 1916.	Capt. A. E. Rann assumed command, *vice* Major H. C. Harrison, gassed.
25th Sept., 1916.	Major H. C. Harrison resumed command.
30th Sept., 1916.	Lt. R. Levy evacuated owing to illness.
22nd Dec., 1916.	Major H. C. Harrison left owing to effects of gas.
22nd Dec., 1916.	Capt. A. E. Rann assumed command.
3rd Jan., 1917.	2nd-Lt. W. J. Davies (R.G.A.) joined the Battery.
17th Feb., 1917.	Bombardier E. W. Bower (71st S.B.) to 75th S.B. as 2nd-Lieutenant.
20th Feb., 1917.	Lt. A. B. Crump transferred to the 73rd S.B. as Captain.
21st Feb., 1917.	Bombardier J. C. Watters (73rd S.B.) to 71st S.B. as 2nd-Lieutenant.
22nd Feb., 1917.	Corporal A. P. Green (73rd S.B.) to 71st S.B. as 2nd-Lieutenant.
7th May, 1917.	Lt. E. J. Lawlor joined the Battery.
7th May, 1917.	2nd-Lt. H. J. Henderson joined the Battery.
9th May, 1917.	Gunner P. D. Waller promoted to 2nd-Lieutenant.
20th July, 1917.	Capt. P. N. G. Fitzpatrick assumed command, *vice* Major Rann, wounded.
25th July, 1917.	Lt. E. J. Lawlor transferred to 73rd S.B. as Captain.
26th July, 1917.	Lt. A. W. F. Roper joined the Battery.
5th Aug., 1917.	Lt. R. Levy rejoined the Battery.
1st Oct., 1917.	Sergeant J. W. Wardrop appointed B.Q.M.S. *vice* B.Q.M.S. T. W. White, gassed.
5th Oct., 1917.	Lt. R. Levy evacuated owing to illness.
5th Dec., 1917.	2nd-Lt. H. C. M. Ross (R.G.A.), 2nd-Lt. N. E. Barrie, and 2nd-Lt. R. J. W. Charlton joined the Battery.

14th Dec., 1917.	Lt. A. W. F. Roper assumed command, *vice* Major Fitzpatrick, killed.
18th Dec., 1917.	Major Hall (R.G.A.) assumed command.
18th Dec., 1917.	2nd-Lt. E. Hancock (R.G.A.) joined the Battery.
12th Jan., 1918.	Major W. Brydon, Capt. R. H. M. Hands, 2nd-Lt. H. Hall and 2nd-Lt. W. Drummond joined the Battery, Major Hall relinquished command to Major Brydon, and left the Battery.
20th Jan., 1918.	B.Q.M.S. Wardrop appointed Acting B.S.M., *vice* B.S.M. Dacombe who left for England. Bombardier I. Isherwood appointed Acting B.Q.M.S.
14th Feb., 1918.	Major E. H. Tamplin assumed command, *vice* Major Brydon, transferred to 73rd S.B.
14th Feb., 1918.	Captain J. R. McCarthy joined the Battery from the 73rd S.B., *vice* Capt. R. H. M. Hands transferred.
3rd Mar., 1918.	2nd-Lt. H. Hall appointed to a commission with the Indian Cavalry.
6th Mar., 1918.	Lt. T. R. Rutherford joined the Battery.
27th Mar., 1918.	2nd-Lt. R. J. W. Charlton seconded to 44th S.A. Brigade.
7th Apr., 1918.	2nd-Lt. W. J. Davies (R.G.A.) transferred to an Imperial Battery.
	Capt. J. R. McCarthy assumed command temporarily *vice* Major Tamplin seconded to 44th S. A. Brigade.
9th Apr., 1918.	B.Q.M.S. G. H. Miles (125th S.B.) appointed B.S.M.
19th Apr., 1918.	Capt. J. R. McCarthy and Lieut. T. R. Rutherford transferred to the 73rd S.B.
21st Apr., 1918.	2nd-Lt. M. E. Wright (R.G.A.) joined the Battery.
28th Apr., 1918.	2nd-Lt. D. Culverwell joined the Battery.
2nd May, 1918.	2nd-Lt. J. V. Brade joined the Battery.
10th June, 1918.	2nd-Lt. F. W. Mellish (73rd S.B.) transferred to 71st S.B.
30th June, 1918.	2nd-Lt. S. B. Gwillam joined the Battery.
17th July, 1918.	2nd-Lt. Gwillam seconded as Instructor to First Corps Artillery School.
4th July, 1918.	Sergeant H. W. Meacham (75th S. B.) appointed B.Q.M.S. *vice* B.Q.M.S. J. Wardrop evacuated owing to illness.
21st July, 1918.	B.Q.M.S. C. G. Duffy (73rd S.B.) appointed B.S.M., *vice* B.S.M. Miles.
27th July, 1918.	B.S.M. G. H. Miles granted a commission in the R.G.A.
23rd Sept., 1918.	2nd-Lt. W. Drummond seconded for duty at Base Depot.
6th Nov., 1918.	2nd-Lt. D. Culverwell evacuated owing to illness.

Casualties.

Ypres, June, 1916. 2nd-Lt. E. Mason severely wounded, 7 other ranks killed, 27 other ranks wounded.

Becordel, August, 1916. Major H. C. Harrison gassed, with 2 other ranks.

Somme, 1916, to August, 1917. Captain A. E. Rann wounded (twice), Lt. E. A. Mitchell wounded severely, 7 other ranks killed, 15 other ranks wounded.

Ypres, September, 1917. Lt. J. C. Watters killed, B.Q.M.S. White gassed, 4 other ranks killed, 25 wounded, and 60 gassed.

Doignies and Beaumetz, December, 1917. Major P. N. G. Fitzpatrick and Lt. P. D. Waller killed, 2nd-Lt. Henderson and 20 other ranks gassed, 5 other ranks killed, and 9 other ranks wounded.

Beuvry and La Bourse, April, 1918. 16 other ranks wounded, 27 other ranks gassed.

Annequin and La Bourse, May, 1918. 4 other ranks wounded and 20 other ranks gassed.

Vermelles, September, 1918. 2nd-Lt. E. Hancock gassed and 17 other ranks gassed.

Coupigny, September, 1918. 1 other rank wounded.

Battery Roll.

2nd-Lt. N. E. Barrie.
2nd-Lt. J. V. Brade.
Major W. Brydon, D.S.O.
Captain A. B. Crump.
2nd-Lt. D. Culverwell, M.C.
2nd-Lt. R. J. W. Charlton.
Lt. W. J. Davies, R.G.A.
2nd-Lt. W. Drummond.
Major P. N. G. Fitzpatrick.
Lt. A. P. Green, M.C.
2nd-Lt. S. B. Gwillam.
Major C. H. Hall, R.G.A.
2nd-Lt. H. Hall.
Lt. E. Hancock, M.C., R.G.A.
Captain R. H. M. Hands.
Major H. C. Harrison, D.S.O.

Lt. H. J. Henderson.
Captain E. J. Lawlor.
Captain R. Levy.
Major J. R. McCarthy.
Lt. F. W. Mellish
Lt. E. Mason.
Captain E. A. Mitchell.
Captain A. W. F. Roper, M.C.
Lt. H. C. M. Ross, R.G.A.
Major A. E. Rann, M.B.E., M.C.
Lt. T. R. Rutherford.
Major E. H. Tamplin, M.C.
Lt. P. D. Waller.
2nd-Lt. J. C. Watters.
2nd-Lt. M. E. Wright, R.G.A.

Abegglen, E.
*Allison, G. H.
Alexander, J.
Allison, F. M.
Allsop, F. R.
Allingham, S.
Anderson, S. C.
Angel, J. F. W.
Arundel, E.
Ashton, J.
Atkins, J.
Austin, R. S.

*Backhouse, W. J.
*Bailey, H. H.
Bailey, B. I. C.
Baldwin, D. H.
Bands, E. W.
Barnard, J. H.
Basson, J. H.
*Beck, J. G.
*Beckman, S.

Begley, P. A.
Benn, W. F.
*Bentley, C.
*Berry, A. J.
*Bergh, D. M.
Benkes, B. M.
*Beveridge, A. J.
*Beyer, W. M.
*Billingham, A.
*Binckes, J. W. T.
Black, W. J.
Black, N.
Bolton, E. C.
*Bower, E. W.
Bowers, H. J.
Bradnum, A. W.
Brent, H. L.
*Bromley, R.
*Brown, J.
*Brown, W. W.
Brown, E.
Brown, A. T.

*Brown, W.
Brown, F. R.
Brown, M.
Brownlee, H. J.
Bruins, W.
*Bryden, R. H.
*Burgess, W. A. R.
Burroughs, T.
Bush, J.
Butler, T. H.

Cahill, J. H.
Calitz, M. C.
Capon, C. H.
*Carbutt, R. L. W.
*Carlyle, T.
Carson, P.
*Cavanagh, T.
**Charlton, R.
Childs, A. E.
Chisholm, R.
*Chittenden, C. G.

Clarke, H. T.
Clarke, H. J.
Clarke, R.
Clegg, J. R.
Cohen, N.
Colclough, J. B.
*Connor, A.
Cook, J.
*Cooper, H. W. A.
Corry C. C.
Cosser, S. C. A.
Cotton, J. W.
*Coughlan, C. G.
*Coull, J.
*Cox, M. B.
*Cox, A. F.
Crighton, J. H.
Crosson, N. R.
Cruickshanks, J. R.

*Dacombe, S. G.
Dallas, A. R.
Damant, C. G.
Daniel, A.
Davids, G. P.
*Davis. W. J.
Deas, G. A.
De Beer, M. A.
De Chaville, E. D. G.
De Klerk, J. A.
De Klerk, I. J.
De Kock, —
De Kock, S. J.
Deetlep, J. P.
De Reuck, S. J.
**De Waal, J. H.
*De Waal, G. J.
Dickson, C. D.
Dickinson, E. B.
*Dorling, T. H.

Dounard, H. D.
*Downing, W.
Dry, R. C.
Duffill, R. E.
Duffy, C. G.
Duffy, P.
Duncan, W.
Du Preez, J. L.

Edwards, E. G.
Edwards, R.
Elliott, G. L.
Ellis, A. W. J.
Ellison, J.
*Ellison, W.
Engela, G.
England, C. A.
**English, J. B.
Everett, F. A.
*Evans, B. J. C.

Fawcett, H. W.
*Fenn, E. D.
**Ferguson, J.
Fergusson, J.
Ferreira, P.
Fisher, M.
Fitzpatrick, H. A. C.
Foster, B.
Foster, G. E.
Foster, H.
Fowler, C.
*Fraser, W. G.
Frieshaar, D. G.

Gallon, E. L.
Galloway, J.
**Gardner, W. T.
*Gay, H. R. G.
Geater, L. E.

Geldhart, J. S.
Giblin, H. J.
Gibson, R. C.
Gilbert, J. T.
Giles, E. H.
Gilfin, W. J.
Glisson, F.
Gordon, A. E.
*Gordon, D.
Gordon, J. E.
*Gordon, P. G.
Gough, C.
*Grassie, J. M.
*Gray, A. J.
Green, A. B.
Green, F. H.
Greenish, H.
Greenwood, H.
Griffin, E. J.
Grœnewald, J. H.
Grœnewald, P. J. H.
*Gull, J. W.

*Hahn, A. F. L.
Hair, C. R. G.
Hall, T. C.
Hamlett, G.
Harding, J. H.
Hardman, H. J.
**Harley, R.
*Harmer, J.
*Harris, G. M.
*Harrison, G. M.
*Harrison, J. G.
Hartland, V. B.
Harty, B. T.
*Hastings, P. E.
*Hawkins, E. J.
Hayes, D.
*Haynes, G. S.

Hayman, W. R.
Hazle, R. G.
Hegter, S. A.
Henson, L. G.
*Henwood, B.
Herschell, D.
Hewitt, S.
Hibbert, W.
*Hickling, J. S.
Hill, R.
Hill, R. E.
Hillman, J. R.
Hincks, H. T.
*Hoare, C. W.
*Hoare, W. S.
*Hocking, W.
*Holland, F.
Holland, M.
**Hopkins, C.
**Hopkins, R.
Horsfall, R. A.
Hosking, R.
House, C. E. V.
*Howard, C. F.
Howe, D. O.
Hulley, H. C.
Hussey, J. H. V.
Hutcheson, J.

*Ifould, F. G.
Iliffe, C. W.
Inman, L. K.
**Isherwood, I.
Isrælstam, G.

*Jackson, T.
Jackson, C.
*Jackson, H.
Jackson, J. E.
*Jackson, M. D.

*Jackson, P. J.
Jacobs, H. C.
James, E. C.
Jay, H. W.
Johnson, J.
Johnson-Robson, W. F.
*Johnston, G. L.
Jones, F.
Jones, H. C.
Jones, S. G.

*Kahn, H. A. H.
Katzen, H.
Keeney, R.
*Kelly, A. E.
Kelly, D. S.
Kelly, F. E.
Keough, M.
Killan, P.
Kilpatrick, W.
**King, G. W.
King, J. M.
Kleinhans, F.
Klerk, F. R.
Koevert, J. H.

Lamond, S.
Laws, A. G.
*Laws, D. J.
Leitch, R.
Lindner, L.
*Little, H. G.
Llewellyn, W. J.
Longbottom, E. H.
*Longstaff, C.
Lowe, R. J.
Lynch, J.

*Mackenzie, P. A.
*Mackie, S. R.

**Mann, H.
Marsh, J. C.
Martin, J.
McAfee, H. G.
*McCarthy, B. I.
McCormack, J.
McDonald, G.
*McDonald, N.
**McGill, J.
McGregor, J.
*McGregor, W. C.
McKinnon, G.
Meacham, H. W.
*Mellish, V.
*Mellors, W. H.
Melvin, J. W.
Meyer, R. M.
Middemost, F. W.
*Middleton, L. V.
Miles, G. H.
*Mills, D. S.
Miller, W. S.
Minter, E. R.
Mitchell, E. A.
Mitchell, R. S.
Monger, L. G.
Moodie, J. A.
*Moore, W. H.
*Morkell, A. V.
*Morrison, W.
*Munro, G. W.
Munro, P. K.
*Murray F. X.
Musquin, B. J.

*Naitby, E.
Neaves, J. C.
*Neill, D. W.
Newman, W. J.
*Nicholson, J.

*Obree, N.
O'Dea, J. S.
*O'Keefe, W. P.
Oppenheimer, O.
O'Keilly, F. J.
*Ormond, J. D.
Otto, W. F.

*Palmer, C. S.
Palmer, W. J. R.
Papenfus, T.
Pargiter, A.
*Pargiter, D.
Parker, C.
*Parker, W.
Parker, H. L.
*Parsons, H. C.
Pascoe, J. C.
Patrick, J.
Pentz, M. P.
Pentz, N. W.
Percival, S. R.
*Perring, J. B.
Peterson, O. L.
**Petters, A. T.
Phillips, C. L.
*Phillipson, W. G.
Pienaar, A. A. de V.
Pierce, E. W.
Pieterse, J. F.
*Pigott, G. F.
Pigott, J. D.
Plenderleith, H. W.
Pretorius, A.
Pretorius, P. G.
*Price, W. H.

Quaile, R. H.

Rattey, E.

Rawbone, J. W.
*Redick, A. W.
*Rennick, H.
*Richards, G. A.
*Richardson, C. J.
Rintoul, H. J.
Riordan, E. R.
Robertson, J. O.
*Robinson, F. R. C.
Robinson, H. E. B.
*Robinson, J.
*Robinson, T.
Rochford, L. J.
Rosser, W.
Rowe, H.
Rubidge, C. J.
Rubidge, F. V.
Ruddle, J. W.

Santer, G. E.
Scallan, J. C.
Schwartz, F. J.
*Senich, L. S. C.
Seruice, W. A.
Shea, L. S. D.
Shirley, C. H. V.
Smith, C. J.
Smith, C. J.
Smith, E. O.
Somers, W.
Souter, A. E.
Southerland, R.
Southern A. W.
Spargo, W. H.
Staats, C. W.
Staples, W.
*Stevens, S. W.
*Stephens, W.
*Stewart, C. W.
**Street, C. C.

Summers, H.
*Symons, G. J. K.

**Tasker, G. T. B.
Taylor, R. H.
Tennant, V.
*Theal, G. M.
Thomas, J.
*Thomas, L. S.
Thompson, R. J.
*Thorburn, A. R.
Thorpe, G.
*Thorpe, L. B.
Thornton, J. H. C.
Thornton, R. W.
Tonkin, N. V.
*Torr, E. H.
Truman, R.
*Turnbull, J. H. M.
Turrel, G. A.
**Twine, L. R.
Twycross, W. D.
Tyser, H. A.

Ueckermann, V.
Ueckermann, W. A.

Van de Merwe, F. C.
Van Eyssen, C. J.
Venter, T.
Vorster, C. A.

*Wade, A.
Wade, J. H.
Walker, G.
*Waller, P. D.
Wells, D.
*Walls, J.
*Wardrop, J. W.
Warne, J. W.

Watkins, G. R.	*Whitcher, E. P.	**Willis, J. V.
Watkins, L. S.	*White, A.	Wilson, J. R.
*Watson, F. A.	*White, G. L. O.	*Winger, J.
Watson, J. S.	**White, L. C.	Witthoft, E. R.
Watt, J.	**White, T. A.	*Wood, C. W.
Watts, F. H. K.	*White, T. H.	Woodgate, A. F.
**Webb, C. S.	*White, T. H.	Worthington, L. G.
*Webb, L. R.	Whitelaw, R. A.	Wright, H.
*Webb, W.	Whitmore, G.	Wright, P. D.
*Wells, S. G.	Widdicombe, R.	
Wells-Blake, W. H.	Wilkie, A. G.	Young, W. R.
Wesson, A. R.	**Williams, A. C.	
*Whalley, E.	Williams, W.	Zeeman, H. J.

(*NOTE*.—One asterisk has been placed against the names of those who came out with the Battery in April, 1916, and a second against the names of such as remained with the Battery up to 11th November, 1918, excepting for periods of leave in the United Kingdom, or periods spent in hospital in France. Some of the members whose names do not bear the second asterisk have left for the O.T.C. or other Batteries.)

PRINTED BY
J. MILES AND CO. LTD.,
68-70, WARDOUR STREET,
LONDON, W. 1.

Lightning Source UK Ltd.
Milton Keynes UK
UKOW05f0131240915

259169UK00014B/499/P